C   y

D0603085

HALLOWEEN

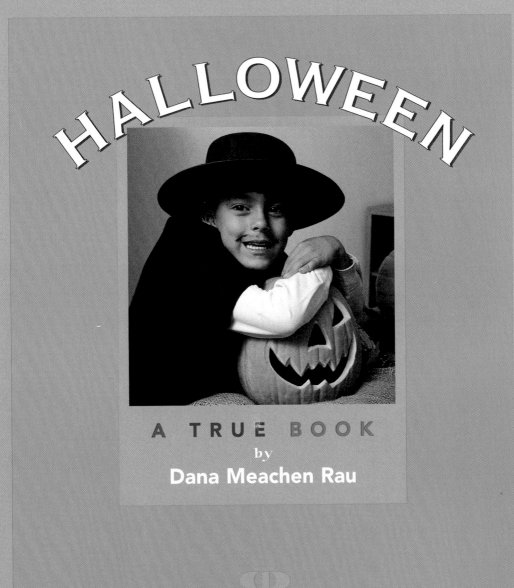

A TRUE BOOK

by

Dana Meachen Rau

Children's Press®
A Division of Scholastic Inc.

New York Toronto London Auckland Sydney
Mexico City New Delhi Hong Kong
Danbury, Connecticut

Jack-o'-lanterns for Halloween

Reading Consultant
Nanci Vargus
Primary Multiage Teacher
Decatur Township Schools
Indianapolis, Indiana

Library of Congress Cataloging-in-Publication Data

Rau, Dana Meachen, 1971-
  Halloween / by Dana Meachen Rau.
      p. cm.–(A true book)
  Includes bibliographical references and index.
  ISBN 0-516-22245-7 (lib. bdg.) 0-516-27347-7 (pbk.)
  1. Halloween—Juvenile literature. [1. Halloween. 2. Holidays.] I. Title.
II. Series.
GT4965 .R33 2001
394.2646—dc21

00-030664

Contents

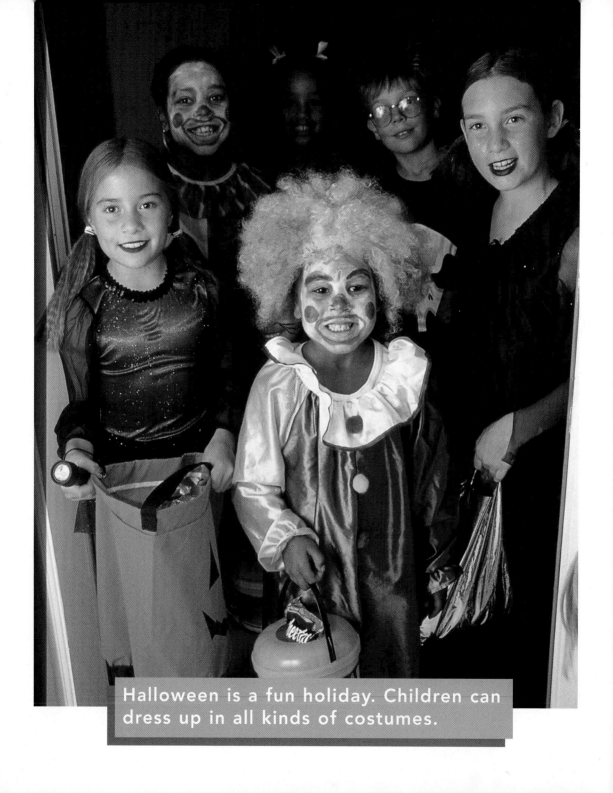

Halloween is a fun holiday. Children can dress up in all kinds of costumes.

Ancient Origins

How do you celebrate Halloween? Do you dress in a silly or scary costume? Do you go trick-or-treating? Do you decorate your house and have a party? Halloween is a fun—and sometimes scary—holiday held every year on October 31.

All of the ways people celebrate Halloween today started as traditions long ago.

Halloween is a combination of celebrations practiced by the ancient Celts and Romans. The Celts lived more than 2,500 years ago throughout what is now called western Europe. October 31 was the last day of the Celtic year. On that day the Celts held a very festive New Year's Eve celebration. It was the beginning of Samhain, like our season of fall. It marked the end of summer and the beginning of winter.

The Celts believed that on October 31 the spirits of loved ones who had died returned to visit their homes. But not only good spirits came out during the holiday. Bad ghosts roamed the countryside making mischief.

The Celts had traditional ways to scare away these

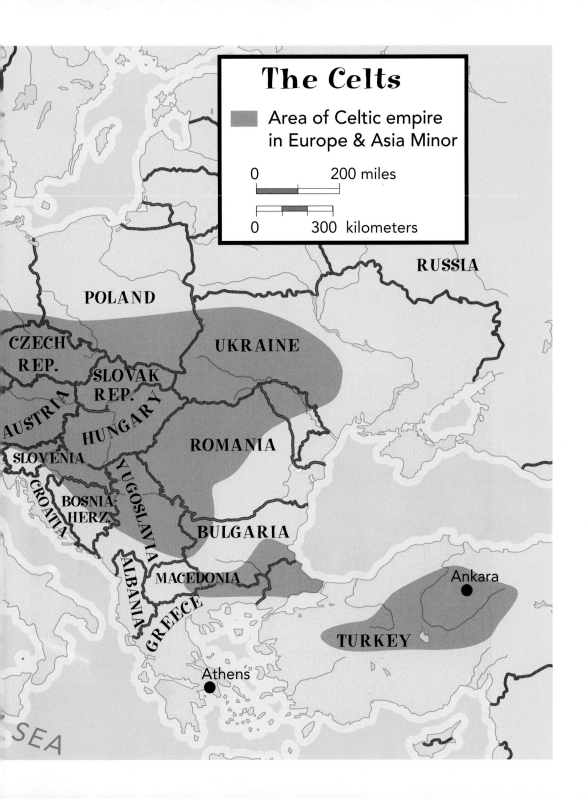

The Celts

Area of Celtic empire
in Europe & Asia Minor

0   200 miles

0   300 kilometers

RUSSIA

POLAND

CZECH
REP.

UKRAINE

SLOVAK
REP.

AUSTRIA

HUNGARY

SLOVENIA

ROMANIA

CROATIA

BOSNIA-
HERZ.

YUGOSLAVIA

BULGARIA

ALBANIA

MACEDONIA

Ankara

GREECE

TURKEY

Athens

SEA

The Celtic cross was an important symbol. As a gravestone, the Celtic cross was a symbol of a home for the spirits of a loved one who had died.

bad ghosts. First, they put out the hearth fires in their homes so that their homes looked cold and empty. They built a large bonfire in the center of town. Then they dressed in scary costumes and masks and danced through the town making lots of noise. They thought this would fool the evil spirits into thinking they were spirits too.

The Celts celebrated this way for five hundred years.

Then the Romans defeated the Celts and took over their land. After this happened, the Romans tried to combine many of the Celtic holidays with their own. The Romans already celebrated a similar holiday in late October called the Feast of Pomona. This day honored Pomona, the goddess of orchards. During this celebration, the Romans gave each other fruit, especially apples, and nuts.

POMONA

Pomona,
the goddess
of orchards

A Christian Holiday

When Christianity began to spread across Europe, the Christians tried to stop the Celts from having their New Year's celebrations. They thought the holiday was unholy and against the teachings of the Christian church. But the Celts refused and would not give up their celebrations. So the Christians created their own holiday based on the Celtic traditions.

The Christians honored saints. To make the New Year's celebrations more Christian, they named the first of November "All Hallow's Day." (Hallow means holy.) On this day they honored all of the saints who didn't have their own holiday. Later, it became

St. Lucy (left) and St. Joan of Arc (below) are Christian saints who are honored by the church for their holy deeds.

known as All Saints' Day. The night before this holiday was called "All Hallow's Eve." Over time, it was shortened to Hallow E'en, and then to Halloween, as we know it. November 2 became known as "All Souls' Day." Like the ancient festivals, it was a day to honor the souls of the dead.

Early Traditions

As time went on, Halloween became very popular in Ireland, England, Scotland, and Wales. Many people were still afraid of ghosts on Halloween. To protect themselves, people wore wreaths of garlic around their necks. They also stayed up all night together and played games.

This wreath of garlic (left) might have hung around someone's neck like a necklace. A young girl bobs for apples (below).

A popular game was bobbing for apples. They filled a large tub with water and apples. Then each person tried to catch the floating apples with their teeth.

Since people believed spirits roamed around on Halloween, some hoped the spirits might be able to tell their futures. For supper on Halloween, Irish families served a dish of potatoes, parsnips, cabbage, and onions called Colcannon. While making the dish, they stirred in a ring and a coin. Whoever found the ring in their serving

These Celtic and Roman coins might have been dropped into the Colcannon.

would marry sometime soon. Whoever found the coin would be wealthy in the future.

The ancient Celts often visited houses asking for money and food for Muck Olla, one of their gods, during the season of Samhain. People in England continued this tradition. On November 2, All Souls' Day, they went "souling." Poor people traveled from house to house to beg for food, asking for "soul cakes," square bread with currants. If they received any, they promised to pray for the people in the family who had died.

As time went on, children went along on these visits and dressed in costumes. They called out "trick-or-treat" as they asked each family for soul cakes. If they didn't receive any cakes, the children would play a trick.

In the United States, people created their own traditions. In the early 1800s, they held play parties. At play parties, people

People still enjoy taking hayrides today.

danced and sang. They ate apples and nuts, and older people tried to scare youngsters with ghost stories. Sometimes people celebrated the fall with corn-popping parties, taffy pulls, or hayrides. By the mid-1800s, thousands of immigrants from England, Ireland, and Scotland made Halloween more popular when they brought their Halloween traditions with them to America.

Have you ever seen candy shaped like a coffin? Have you ever bought skull-shaped bread in a bakery? You can find them both in Mexico on All Souls' Day, November 2.

All Souls' Day is called the Day of the Dead, and it is a major national holiday in Mexico.

Mexicans like to decorate their food with scary symbols, like this skull cake.

Children go trick-or-treating.

the Dead

Women pray by candle-light in front of the graves of loved ones in Mexico.

Families visit cemeteries and have picnics near the graves of their loved ones. It is a very happy and festive day when people think about members of their family.

Women in traditional Mexican dresses wear white masks on the holiday.

Spooky Symbols

Witches are one of the most common Halloween symbols. People used to believe that witches rode through the sky causing trouble.

Some animals are symbols of Halloween, too. Pictures of owls, bats, and black cats can be found decorating houses

Black cats, owls, and ghosts are favorite symbols on Halloween.

during the holiday. Long ago, the Celts believed evil spirits came back as black cats, or that witches changed into cats on All Hallows' Eve for easy travel.

People were not always scared of ghosts. They believed a visiting ghost might be the spirit of a dead relative. Families invited ghosts into their homes and "fed" them a large meal.

They believed that if they didn't leave out enough food, the ghost might play tricks on them.

Jack-o'-lanterns remind everyone of Halloween. In Ireland, people once carved jack-o'-lanterns to protect themselves from evil spirits. They hollowed out the insides of small turnips, carved faces outside, and put candles inside.

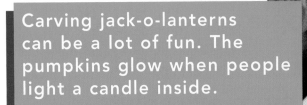

Carving jack-o-lanterns can be a lot of fun. The pumpkins glow when people light a candle inside.

Why are they called jack-o'-lanterns? The story is that a long time ago an Irishman named Jack played a lot of

tricks on the devil. When
Jack died, Heaven didn't
want to take him in. The devil
didn't want him either

because Jack had tricked him so many times. So Jack was doomed to wander the Earth holding a lantern to light his way.

Turnips are no longer carved for jack-o'-lanterns. Instead, most people carve pumpkins. When the Irish came to America, they found that pumpkins were ripe around Halloween and made better lanterns than small turnips did.

Halloween Today

Over the years, Halloween traditions have changed with the times, but many are still like those of the past. Today, children go trick-or-treating, much like children used to go souling in England. Instead of asking for soul cakes, children ring

Some children carry the UNICEF box while trick-or-treating. They help collect donations for poor and hungry children.

doorbells, say "trick-or-treat," and receive candy. Since 1965, some children collect money for the United Nations International Children's Fund (UNICEF). UNICEF gives the money to poor and hungry children around the world.

You might see children dressed as superheroes, animals, princesses, or robots. You can even make a costume yourself. You just need felt ears and a tail to be a cat, or a sheet with two eye-holes to be a ghost.

Some children go to Halloween parties held by friends or their teachers at school. Parties may include costume parades or contests where children win prizes for the scariest, silliest, or most original costumes. Children eat caramel apples and carve pumpkins.

Apples are also an important part of celebrations in England. There, Halloween is sometimes called Nutcrack Night or Snap Apple Night. People munch on nuts, sit by the fire, and tell scary stories. They might play a game of "snap apple" by hanging an apple from a string. While the apple sways, they try to catch it with their teeth.

On Halloween children might have a party at school, go to a costume parade, or go trick-or-treating.

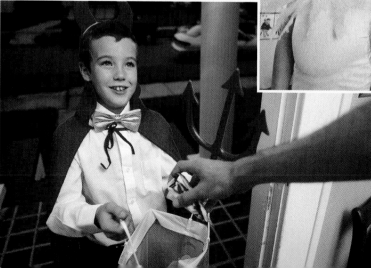

Halloween is celebrated mostly in the United States, Canada, England, Scotland, Wales, and Ireland. No matter how you celebrate, it is a chance to hang spooky decorations, act scared, and imagine you are someone or something else by dressing in a costume. Halloween is a fun time for pretending!

Halloween Safety

If you go trick-or-treating on Halloween, it is important to be safe. Here are some tips to remember:

1. Take an adult with you and only visit houses of people you know.

2. Wearing makeup is safer than wearing a mask because it is easier for you to see.

3. If you do wear a mask, be sure the eyeholes are large. Please take it off when you have to cross the road.

4. Be sure your costume is nonflammable. Also, be sure it is bright enough to be seen in the dark. If it isn't, wear reflective tape.

5. Be sure your costume isn't too long. You don't want to trip on it.

6. Don't eat any candy until an adult checks through it.

To Find Out More

Here are some additional resources to help you learn more about Halloween and other holidays:

 **Books**

Chambers, Catherine. **All Saints, All Souls, and Halloween.** Raintree Steck-Vaughn Publishers, 1997.

Corwin, Judith Hoffman. **Halloween Crafts.** Franklin Watts, 1995.

Hintz, Martin, and Kate Hintz. **Halloween: Why We Celebrate It the Way We Do.** Capstone Press, 1996.

Roop, Peter, and Connie Roop. **Let's Celebrate Halloween.** The Millbrook Press, 1997.

Organizations and Online Sites

Festivals.com
RSL Interactive
1101 Alaskan Way
Pier 55, Suite 300
Seattle, WA 98101
http://www.festivals.com

Visit this site to find out about all types of festivals, holidays, and fairs around the world.

The Holiday Page
http://wilstar.com/holidays

Find out about your favorite celebrations at this web site, which is devoted to holidays throughout the year.

UNICEF
3 United Nations Plaza
New York, NY 10017
http://www.unicef.org

UNICEF is devoted to helping children around the world. At this site, find out what you can do to help them in their mission.

Important Words

ancient very, very old, or from very early in history

bonfire a very large fire

hearth the area in front of the fireplace

immigrant a person who moves to a new country

mischief playful behavior that may cause annoyance or harm to others

sacred something that is holy

saint a person who lived a good and holy life, or one who died for his or her religious beliefs

soul cake a square piece of bread with currants

symbol an object that stands for something else

tradition a custom, an idea, or a belief that is passed through history

Index

Meet the Author

Ever since Dana Meachen Rau can remember, she has loved to write. A graduate of Trinity College in Hartford, Connecticut, Dana works as a children's book editor and has authored many books for children, including biographies, nonfiction, early readers, and historical fiction. She has also won writing awards for her short stories.

When Dana is not writing, she is doing her favorite things—watching movies, eating chocolate, and drawing pictures—with her husband, Chris, and son, Charlie, in Farmington, Connecticut.